The

JANE DRAYCOTT was born in 1954. She has worked as a teacher, living in London, Tanzania, Strasbourg and, most recently, Oxfordshire, where she has been poet in residence at Henley's River and Rowing Museum.

Also by Jane Draycott from Carcanet/Oxford*Poets*

Prince Rupert's Drop

JANE DRAYCOTT

The Night Tree

Oxford*Poets*

CARCANET

First published in Great Britain in 2004 by
Carcanet Press Limited
Alliance House
Cross Street
Manchester M2 7AQ

A CIP catalogue record for this book is available from the British Library
ISBN 1 903039 72 X

The publisher acknowledges financial assistance from Arts Council England

Set in Monotype Bembo by XL Publishing Services, Tiverton
Printed and bound in England by SRP Ltd, Exeter

for Norman, Holly and Sophie
and in memory of Peter Hay

Acknowledgements

Thanks are due to the editors of the following publications in which some of these poems first appeared: *The Guardian*, *The Independent*, *Oxford Poetry*, *Oxford Poets 2001* (Carcanet/OxfordPoets), *Poetry London*, *The Rialto*, *The Times Literary Supplement*, www.boomerangUK.com, www.poetrysoc.org.uk, the 2000 and 2002 Bridport Prize anthologies and *The 2002 Forward Book of Poetry*.

'No. 3 from Uses for the Thames' was a postcard commission for Southern Arts Year-of-the-Artist 2000/1. 'An Alchemy' was commissioned by Southern and South East Arts for Christmas 2002. An original version of 'The Lost Girls' was written for the Commonplace Book celebrating thirty years of publishing by Carcanet Press (2000). 'The Night Tree' was winner of the Keats–Shelley Poetry Prize 2002 and first published in *The Keats–Shelley Review*. The poems from *Tideway* (Two Rivers Press 2002, illustrated by Peter Hay; www.tworiverspress.com) were written during a Year-of-the-Artist residency at the River and Rowing Museum, Henley on Thames.

The opening line of 'Fossil Collector' is taken from Shelley's 'Summer and Winter'. 'Channel' includes extracts from the River and Rowing Museum audio archive and *A Time of Gifts* by Patrick Leigh Fermor.

My grateful thanks are especially due to Southern Arts (now part of Arts Council England South East) and The Authors' Foundation (Society of Authors) for their support and generous financial assistance.

Contents

from *Tideway*

The Night Tree

Secondly there are the beams or sails
sometimes called petals or branches
which on account of their reaching out
through all the timetables of dark
we are forever working to maintain
and which passing vessels have likened
to the after-death appearances of saints
or the ashes of great seafarers set up
as a beacon at the gate of a new land
where like a mermaid a ship
would be surely certain to founder.

Next there is ourselves, each man
on his watch for the deception of fog
or shudder of the tower,
each keeping awake in his turn
for the sake of the light by his reading
of Plutarch's *Parallel Lives*, our one book
relayed on the stairs between watches,
or else in the pinning of moths flattened
like leaves on the lantern whose wings
like a searchlight come sweeping our walls
finding each of us out in our beds.

But first as I say there is the sea
which is a forest, our blades
cutting through like a photograph,
a sequence of light and dark pathways,
hourglasses, rain, where time travels slowly
as if at great height or in exile and men
report voices heard crying in darkness,
though for myself I think it is only the seals
calling to each other in their language
through all the leafiness of the night.

What is held here

What is held here, weighing so little, keeps
close to the floor and where linoleum gives way
to wilderness, gathers in the shadows of stones.

The days pass like thieves in the disinfection
of letters, the collective study of quarantine law
and the microscopic recitation of sand.

At the doors experts assemble for discussion
of germ theory and scum, and all the while night
like a ship at bay waits to present itself ashore

to pitch its tent of stars, the dome of its hammam
on which are printed all the ancient maps
of the lazaretto and the echo of your name in writing.

Beyond the window the world looks like a dream
where other men row their boats freely, turn
stones into bread, walk to the shops. Welcome.

Because tonight the beach

Because tonight the beach will consider its life,
its lack of a future, tree hair thinning
and tree heart turning to stone or splinters of ice

they will arrive now, the snow girls, swimming in
from their islands, weightless detonations of paper or marble
or light, casting no shadows and wearing no shoes.

Not asking what country, whose footsteps or features or fable,
they'll travel together like raiders, sending the ghosts
of previous weather curling across the dunes

feathering stonework and fences, their deepening presence
an absence, a plainness of speech laid on car parks and lawns,
a glimpse of a possible future, making a difference

to everything, this arrival of strangers, now –
familiar, unblemished, and just the right age for snow.

The Gardens

Watch how dusk slips into the vegetable gardens
to wait in company with the thirteen apricots
braced against the espalier wall, the steel-green leeks,
the undefended corn, for locust night's platoon.

At the school this morning's singing remains
behind in the hall, is lying very still on the floor.
On Liberation Street dogs chase a formless stranger
in their midst, the stones surrender up their heat.

Beyond the town's thin walls the mandrake cries
of distant gardens are now clearly audible,
whole houses used for lanterns, forests half-asleep
with snow ordered to dig their own graves.

Sunrise hits the school wall first. The dark swarms
trickle from the kitchens. Into the land of the living
from cellars where all night they've lain like toppled
columns on the earth, the children emerge.

Boy

He remembers wearing the fish dress, opening
the door to the yard like a book on the forces of weather
and seeing them there, a downpour of fingerlings

silvery, gasping for air, laid at his feet like a cloth
flung out from the bolt, like something arranged in advance.

He remembers imagining them lifted, a miraculous
draught to be held in the sky for a day and a night
then dropped from the clouds like the back of a truck

or the falling folds of a lake into which one might
easily sink or survive by the action of swimming.

He remembers his father whose question was
have you no shame, the answer he gave being
no, there was none to be had but look at the fish.

At the Party

for Norman

At the party everyone must speak
about how they arrived there: the road-works,
the sheet-ice like linen, the tangerine cones.
This man gesturing gently is speaking
of the Great West Road, the fruit he dreamed of
as he motored past the exhausted farms
and dried-up garages, the abandoned
Traveller's Rest and all the Halfway Houses,
the town which showed as a low orange glow
in the sky but never appeared on the road,
the fox curled up in the fast lane trying to sleep.
He is on his way to spend the evening
with his daughters somewhere circular and light –
the end of a tunnel maybe, or an orchard.

Blue

Some thought they heard *flight*, others
that *fight* was the syllable uttered
on the floor of the forest, the young man
far from home, unable to tell us even his name.

All afternoon those among us convinced
they knew the root of a word when they saw it
argued the toss between *agony* and *ecstasy*

the green of his jacket the whole while dividing,
bursting towards the light, his mouthful of soot
spat upward in a fountain of feathers or leaves.

Night fell. We bent to the bones, hoping to hear
like the Bible translated against all laws
some sounds we might more easily swallow.
Kneeling, we listened.

Night driving

in unknown country, the burning car
on the slip road already in the rear-view,
Moscow, Hilversum, Allouis, Prague,
the back seat lit up like a torched city

then what sounds like a play about airmen
night training, an ad for a theme park,
an SOS shot in the dark for a woman
on holiday currently thinking she's free

and three fields away the headlong race
of a river running for years across Europe
without stopping or once looking back,
Home, Light, Third, home, light, home

and there again on the hour is the story
that won't bear repeating, returning again
like the name of the ill-fated village you'd swear
you passed on the dial several hours ago

with its riots and ribs of what looks like cloud
though it's hard to make out so we turn on
the local storm warning – *fast and feast, beauty
and the beast, ahead, in the rear-view and burning.*

Set like a net

Set like a net for the shadows of telegraph poles
falling over themselves to get home before dark,
this old system of fields receives its dead.

Raising themselves like light, the circus people
imagine themselves, sewing on stars, walking
the wires, crossing the high pass to safety.

The news will barely have reached us before it's all over,
the juggling of children and plates, the throwing of torches,
the hanging of fathers and sons by their feet in the spotlight.

In the hedgerows the old men fine-tune their breath
to a filament, listening in to the silence of travellers
catching each other, putting a hand out tonight.

Pale

for Pete

Inside this shepherds' church your bed floats
through winter and each wall's a single day.
Beneath the limewash, laths and batons mark
the hours your light's suspended on. You dream
of what an X-ray might reveal: the bare bones
of a landscape, pale saints like newborn animals
before their adult coat, an almost invisible man.

You have parked the car beyond the fence, allowing
the wind to carry you through these Early English doors.
The font's an eggcup or a bowl in which you'll wash
the darker colours from your brush before you leave
striding out past day-lilies, the child with the head
of an angel, across the boundary field for home.

Up at the House

So sorry if I have offended you
by that poem up at the big house
sorry eaten at the edges is discovered
behind the gun cabinet, a small intense thing
requiring all their powers of detection.

I just put down the first thing that come
to me beyond the formal garden
a birch wood of nervy pathways is seen
striking out across the field line,
thin limbs fired by an unexpected sun.

If it isn't the poem that has upset you,
what has that poem which is
so hungry, that cabinet so curious about
what's locked away and who is who,
the power of fire and motives gone astray.

You glare at me as if I'd committed
a murder. Please burn this together
with all records of whatever's happening.
On no account leave it to smoulder
or hold it near to your body or ear,
the most dangerous thing in the house.

The italicised text is from a note found during work at The Vyne (National Trust)
in Hampshire.

Matchless

1   The Lost Girls

Lost to their fathers flawless
and small they slip, Margery
Rita and Pearl, into sleep
one August embankment
all gates locked, laughing, leaving.

Across the water distant
and dream–led wander the men
cliff-faced by crystal and quartz,
splendid as winter, forested,
following the girls with their eyes.

In their dreams they are diving
for faces pale as perfection
searching the stream-beds and streets,
the forests of flyovers,
deeper and deeper they dive.

Each imagines on waking
he's found her, the woman
he knows is only a child
set like a lamp by a river,
lifting the phone to ring home.

2   The Jeweller

Around her steam slides silking
the gutter as she behind glass
shoves coins to kick the message
home: she's great on her own, can't
wait to get out of the box.

From the current of cables
he cups up her voice, weighing
his loss in his hands from where
like a seed she has fallen
his jewel lost in the grass.

Not fallen here but flying
like Sindbad landed alone
on the hill the other side
of the happiness valley,
its high invisible shore.

She through separation's smoke
can hear the jeweller calling,
that far voice outstretched to grasp
his pearly queen, his daughter,
girl who is already air.

3   Out in the Twilight Zone

Blown like cloud down the boardwalks
and reaches, loose limbed, dateless,
spun in the limitless wind –
all roads open eight till late,
this is the time of their lives.

Evening comes on in houseboats
and hotels, the upside-down
world reappears where less luck
is more luck, darkness is light
and last on the list might be first.

Out all night, flecks in the wash
of police boats, the river's
their guide to life beyond home –
cold, fast, a wide enough wound
to drag them any distance.

At last sleep falls on the steps
of offices in whose files
if they looked they'd only find
themselves innocent. Streets off
the men stop, straining to hear.

4   The Towers

Morning matchless hits the fire
escapes, contact prints the day
she will wake to: the creeping
sense that someone has taken
her photograph while she slept.

Then rain and helicopters
hung like body bags from blades
cross the city, radio down
the news from the other side
it looks like hell down there.

At last the towers shift, lift
their shadows to leave less night
in kitchens and missions. Charged
with one half-life the voices
of girls gather like water.

On cloudless paper they write:
*these shadows, this waterside
dreaming's a region we can't
be brought home from*, their words
torn sidelong under the bridge.

5   The Bridge

On gold cold streets each alley's
both exit and entrance, doors
blind to the scatter of silver
at their feet, apostle spoons
laid sleeping there, losing shine.

That poverty is purity,
the lie. In the river's reach
it all started and stumbling
will end, no sun no moon bright
enough to bring her to light.

From his refuge on the bridge
each girl in gatherings of girls
marks minutes of might-be-her
before delight dives, drowns.
Now dawn not willing to wait

draws his dream from him, rests it
a while on the water, pale
oars passing in pools, footsteps
on the surface dissolving
pleasing only to others.

Holmes Receives his Fellowship
from the Royal Society of Chemistry

He appears for a moment to fade, lost
in the fog which encircles his head.
The microphone leans towards him
like a question shouted into the wind
Who are you waiting for on such
a freezing night? Areas of his brain
are needles of fire, clear signals across
open ground. The carpet rolls its red road
out across the centuries of snow.
And what is it you fear so greatly?
Disembodied mind swirls in free-fall
beyond the window pane, frost calculates
its way across the floor. *As you value*
your reason, keep away from the moor.

How he knew he was turning to glass

By the curvature of the earth's spine
visible through his shoes.
By the icicle noises made by messengers
arriving with news of battle.
By the feathers.

By the playing like wind in his hair of exhalations
from the distant leper colony.
By the images of himself repeated in the candelabras
of his erections.
By the dark water.

By the constellations left behind with particles
of pink and green on the bathmat.
By his flying at night over gardens of coral
blossoming like surgeons' blades.
By the coldness of his feet.

By the writing in the air above the shoulders
of certain of his friends.
By the misty appearance at dusk of seven stars
best seen by looking away.
By the piles of sand.

The Diagrams

Under his fingers the book spreads itself
wider. Like the legs of spiders working
to explain the shape of things, the diagrams
gaze in his direction. They do not sit there
worrying about the future or losing hope.

His mother hovers like an icon in the corner
where she thinks the devil and his virus wait –
Beelzebub, lover of right angles, of walls
which join and go their separate ways
immediately, of girls who'll do the splits.

The study heats by slow degrees.
His father fills the room with saucers,
keys which turn full circle in the lock,
photos of the great eclipse (the brief
exploding solitaire, the cuts upon its face).

He knows that when the book is closed
the diagrams pass their coded messages
in silent Chinese whispers uncorrupted
to the final page, then lie like lovers
looking at each other in the dark.

He'd like to climb inside them, like climbing
out a window to a field of mist, a place
where mind's not agitated, an empty bed
in which to lie invisible, the eye of God,
a nothing hung in the centre of a triangle.

Fossil Collector

It was a winter such as when birds die
and ice on their wings the old forget
themselves in downstairs rooms.

Along the edges of airfields,
beneath the high cabins of travellers,
the wasted cry of the curlew and the loon.

At midnight, hinged and stretched
to vanishing point and no one
allowed to sleep, he imagined them:

Everest's sea-creatures swimming again,
the bathers in the desert caves
taking one last additional stroke.

Outside his window a cabaret
of tropic birds below the water level,
a dripping hawthorn tree, a flood.

At dawn the candles grow cold, the fish
stiffen in the ponds, the wood-pigeons
sing again and again *You must remember this*.

Transformer

Under his hat they were certain was where
he kept the cables, coils and metal core
contained between the crown and crazy hair.
What they couldn't see was the picture
he had of himself each night without the hat,
stripped naked in a cage round which a ball
of lightning played, throwing itself at his heart
as moonlight throws a window to the floor.

By day what he kept in view was his stride,
small feet carrying his whole down pavements
and across fields like a river carried
in the mouths of fish, alternate movements
pacing out electric night, stepped down,
made bearable for factory and home.

Lay

Land falls between you and me,
a hard place where the stone is deaf
and the face of the rock is set.
Water colours the walls and cathedrals
and rain like the angel stands with one foot
in the sea. In the place where you are
your song works on light-towers,
abbeys and headstones of fishermen
caught by the weather the wrong side
of lucky, coming in like the man who slept
for a night and woke to a day twenty years
down the coast and the news that his parents
unable to wait had entered the hillside
or tunnel without him. Fissure, friable, falling.

The Road

Travellers leaving their horses overnight at the prehistoric burial site of
Wayland's Smithy believed they would find them newly shod by morning.

Full once of the kind of folk you might well hope
to meet, this field or street's deserted, empty
even of footprints. Of the ancient shoe by the side
of the road, of the articles dropped and of the suitcases
no sign or symbol at all. More than the question of oaks
or beeches, their age or purpose, is the wordless army
of fence posts, the deliberate mist which gathers at night,
frost's covert displacing of stones from the rockface.

And now here's this turn in the weather: the storms
which arrive like a shipwreck from nowhere, the consequent wait
in a lifeboat, tipped like a cup to the lip of the tide,
the stowaways eyeing their feet, spectral and blue with
the distance they've travelled, shoeless and hopeful, from home.
All the locals are able to say is that promises made
have yet to be kept, that firing starts around midnight
and travellers passing will sometimes make offerings or music.

The Note

To the monks in their cells and the dumbstruck,
to the prisoners in solitary and those with no voice
National Day of Silence dawned like any other.

Everyone else prepared for long walks or hours
of writing or painting. In the hills the four winds
gathered like tributaries, an assembling of clans.

By eleven most people were listening like spies,
scanning the unspoken airwaves like birds
circling the winter branches of trees.

With the first gusts old leaves filled the sky
and in the streets citizens stood frozen, pinned
by an inchoate thought at the back of the throat.

Like water on a rock or gales around a drystone wall
others surged on past, each tuning in to the note,
a rising river or advancing army from a long way off,

a single note made by everything best left unsaid.
And when the time came to speak and tears filled
their eyes everyone agreed a day was not enough.

On the Island

At the heart of the island a funeral is taking place.
Heat lays its hand again upon the shoulder
of the mountain and from a library of flame trees
the last thoughts dreamed by the deceased
are broadcast in a flowering magnetic field.
Dragonflies rise like fever words from the mouth
of the volcano, weak signals from a far-off core.

Down at the coast in the fish bars and residences
the radios cast their nets, the citizens stare to sea.
After their tears they dance together to forget.
In the hills the mourners gather at the station
grateful for any train in the right direction
away from the cold lips of the caldera.

The Guava Path

Above him the blue and the fist
of the forest pulling the darkness
into itself like a handkerchief.
When weighed in the balance
one foot is as good as the other
but day is always better than night.

All this madness leaves the boy cold –
the reddening pathways, foreign
and uncontrolled, the morning's
outright humidity, the village free-falling
behind him, forgotten already.

He is climbing the stairs to the rock
which faced with the sea is a child
and has waited up for him all night.
He would like to lie down there,
to sleep like a baby right through the day,
but knows that all he can do

is stare at his wall for sight of the girl
when she comes, of the ship
which will move like an institution,
an impossible knot on the silken cord
of horizon, bringing her to him,
making them known to everyone.

Not the sky but the sea. Not the me but the you.
Not the I but the we. Not the blue but the blue.

Cockermouth Boy

In the museum's volcanic dark light dark
the stuttering boy raises the aerial of his arm
and offers to read: *And in – the – frosty – season,*
pushing the blades of the words out across
the surface of the morning, left right left,
each iron phrase a forward movement of himself.

Outside the rain wheels and fills the conduits
and lakes, gathering like wax. *All – shod with – steel*
we hissed – along the – polished – ice, the schoolboy
pitching the whole body of his intonation into the skirts
of the wind, each sound caught, delayed, relayed.

Behind him, close to his ear, the poet's arcing skates
and sunlight pooled in the mouth of the clouds.

The Tor

Coming down she met the others coming up,
moving together like eggs in a basket
or thoughts she'd once had while walking home from school.

They looked like total strangers now, pale and grey.
She wondered if that was how she'd looked: climbing
through cloud to what they imagined must be sun.

She wanted to tell them how at the summit
it was raining, snowing, too windy to stand,
that all she desired now was to walk back home
the way she'd come and read about them by the fire.

But none of them was listening – together
they stared ahead to the top, the strange tower
whose purpose no one knew, and hidden from view
what might have been lightning, flashing, turning, blue.

The Suitcase

Two is all she's permitted: here and there.
Labelled in permanent ink to prevent the weather
from mispronouncing her name.

Eyewitness accounts all speak of the street
leading up from the dock as reliably sunny
on one side at least and busy with people
arriving and leaving, a case in each hand –

an overnight bag for taking one day at a time
and a suitcase bulging with mountains or forests,
or even in one case a beach with waves spilling out
at the corners and voices preserved in the sand.

However she fills it, she knows that the suitcase
will one day prove totally empty on opening
like the candlestick set on the family table
will one day be only herself face to face with herself.

She does not know what will happen tomorrow,
which side of the street she'll wake up on.

Movable Feast

Coming to the table she could see them slipping away,
the mountains of winking olives, the platefuls of painted eggs
sure as onions off to that wild country in the middle of next week
where she with her outstretched hand had no wish to follow.

Slipping their moorings like icebergs or certainties
in the gentlemen's excuse-me, the fatted calf and the leg
of lamb tangoed their way down the hallway leaving her standing,
the kitchen coming and going like a mirage in the afternoons.

It all hung on the moon, on an upstairs room, this retreat
of fishes and loaves, of placenames and settings
decamping with all the energy of despair from where she knew
she last saw them, was something she always saw coming.

Soon she would turn the gas onto its back, would pour
tomorrow into the flat pan and throw it towards the sky.

The Cupboard

From here it is six paces to the cupboard,
one for each continent, and in the cupboard
are the shoes, hidden there like two ears
in the dark against the arrival of ill fortune.

She has heard of people who like to wear
loud shoes, red shoes and glass slippers
dancing at night bus stops and under blind windows
where half-drowned by dreams others are trying to sleep.

But she would rather be a passenger on a plane
travelling the world with her shoes off, or living
in the canopy with apes whose feet don't touch
the forest floor from the day they are born until death.

She approaches it as quietly as humanly possible,
curling her toes like an athlete on the earth's floor.
She knows that in the night the shoes are listening
for warning of the day she has to run.

The Wheel of Cheese

Moon. Sun. Inscribed upon its skin
each infant's avalanche of cries
(the day, the year), the violent storms,
the rising water level of the died,
the numbered count of miracles,
arrivals of a stranger, names of those
who scrambled up beyond the fossil-line.
Then taken from the dark of the pantry
(where today the living stream still runs
beneath the floor), up the glacier
and rolled like a gift into the next valley.

Single Lens

i.m. D.H.P.

1   The Valley

The sheep's-eye view: a pile of houses
crumbles like a great white cheese
gone over, and moss lives in the air.

The stone-cold drains, clean as spit,
lie on their backs by the side of the road
and laugh. The throat of the valley.

In the windows lace turns to chainmail.
Buried alive in the stonework the televisions
ramble, the back parlours mumble their beads.

The roofs collect like sand in the spine
of a book. From the hill, every grain is clear
as daylight. Look up to the man on the hill.

2   The Hill

Still furled inside your camera
your last few hours bide their time.
Eventually they will have to come out
and collide with what we now know:

that within the outstretched arms
of the valley the evening had agreed
with the purple-shouldered mountain
on a landscape that would last you forever.

That this was your perfect place,
from which no dreamer wakes,
the grass and the flowers of the field
crying out to be recorded.

How were you to know, looking out
and leaning on the elbow of the hill,
that the place was giving you
its last and final showing?

3   The House

We have opened the front door
and already the hallway is shouting
how all of our days are diminished.
The furniture stands insolently the same.

Is the wind which inhabits your drying clothes
what you now are? Collapsed
and purged, they are returned
to wait in the dark of the drawer.

4   The Road

Across a field of rain a blackened castle
sheers into low cloud. Beside us as we drive
its stone rises like a cooling tower, rim lipped
with cumulus, skirts runnelling with water.

We are unable to locate you beyond this,
that you have gone with the men who rode down
in the rain, into the past which is one place.

Field Hospital

Each sheet has its own length.
A few are only a short afternoon,
others stretch for what seems like an eternity
all the way to the fence and the several
remaining fields just visible beyond.
Packets of voices pass overhead
held in the shifting nets of the rain.
Lying in the cool straightforward grass
no one can see their toes or needs to:
the horizontal wraps them up and delivers them
to the sky who will say *yes lie down, sleep*
and I will observe you for as long as it takes.

Heron

For a while you may imagine yourself
a heron rising from the pools of mud
legs trailing like spent smoke home

or in the far blue catch the ripped skirt
of the Channel tattering its threads
on the wire before you enter the maze.

Think of your blindness as with you
since birth. You will find yourself able
to visualise objects you have never seen:

women with the patience of trees,
signposts frozen with longing,
a detailed ground-map out of this hole.

Down every alley you will be followed
by a blustering wind. This is the tribe.
Your only view will be the phases of sky.

At every dead-end there will be fires
and men working a field. Continue turning
until you come to a white road. Take it.

Inside the Glasshouse

for Peter Scupham

Under the sky's light, this bank of seeds.
Each is a two-way mirror, an eye raised
to the weather, an ear held to the ground.

Then greater than glass the wind,
a door burst open, the vaulting dash
to the wild. First thyme then willow then ash.

Sundial

folded like the dark heart
of the artichoke inside its box

its broken daylight a crack
in a wall or a door half-shut

against the coming of the gardener,
the tell-tale heart or hearth

the walk to the morning
the other end of the path

An Alchemy

All morning they worked together at bringing them in,
veils of sea-mist like white lead spun to a whisper,
acres of frost on iron-sung dockyards and downs,
light-miles of mercury drawn from the cold canals.

Everyone watched as the sun transmuted the load
distilled not as gold but as glass, an alternative world
inscribed in the curvings of light – an odyssey
caught in a bottle, the spire in the eye of a horse.

That evening they watched again at the feet of the sea,
its leave-taking tide transformed by the moon to a point
of precious arrival, wave upon wave coming inland,
not turning back, silvery, travelling, turning to mist.

from
Tideway

Salvage

At his heels all the bigger rooms –
day, night, air – have closed their doors
as blindfold he enters the attic of the water.

Like particles of sleep mud raises itself
to his mask, and with his mind's eye
he fingers the darkness for signs of her.

This is the underworld of the deliberately lost,
the unforeseen consequence, MOT failure or weapon,
the barges for whom the river has all got too much.

Draped in silt, the debris delivers itself
to his fingertips, soft as the edges of thought,
as a handbrake left off, as the key to a previous door.

Far off he hears the approaching engine
of her name, a deep chest knocking. In his hand
the blue flame flowers and he begins to cut.

Slowly he surfaces and in the empty air
of the house the river runs off his face like a song.

Public Records Office

If you would see something quite dreadful, go to the enormous palace in the
Strand, called Somerset House ...What can men do in such a catacomb?

Taine, *Notes sur l'Angleterre*

Ink comes in on the tide and with the watermen
and moths cuts up the stairs. Witnesses crowd
the courtyard in pairs, details are lost in the rain.

Behind the dead windows darkness is swallowing
the *Aula lucis*, the hall of light, like a sword:
year by year, marriage by marriage, a steady hand.

Last night, another murder in the water gardens.
Torches doused, the facts sit in pools on the flags
and that blind old allegory the Thames refuses to speak.

No mention here of those unaccountably let off
the hook, of the dates they were not with their friends
in the runaway hackneys, the train wrecks

or warships which broke like a biscuit, cordite
gangfiring back like a family tree through torpedo room,
ocean, the North Sea, past sandbanks and home.

In the river the house and its offices hang like a ship
smeared with soot and the memory of flame underwater.

Surgeon

He swims just before dawn, breasting the river
like a hill, parting it with his arms like a dancer
or priest. Ahead, a flat line of light divides
the two dark halves of the world from each other.

The air leans up to his face and with his ears only
he senses the dark landscape of the water,
its prostrate fields and struggling hedges,
its low-lying ridges and flooded verges.

Below the surface pearls of half-light, silver
with oxygen, cling like prayer beads to his fingers.
He is thinking about the anatomy of the heart,
the forks in the road, the red caves and narrow lanes

and on the horizon the possibility of a cathedral,
the sun rising like a corpuscle, winter wheat.

No. 3 from *Uses for the Thames*

'*Feather!*' *cried the Sheep ...*
Lewis Carroll, *Through the Looking-Glass*

The test was to dip
the needles into the dark
of the swallowing mirror

and by pulling to row
the weight of your own small self
through the silvery jam of its surface

trailing behind in your passing
your very own tale, knitted
extempore from light

and then to lift them,
feathered, ready for flight.

St Mary Overie

To Mary over the ferry
a single ticket taken,
to press the features into the pale
beyond the body of this water.

To Slut Lane let him be carried
a pilgrim by the boatman
led by the spill of the vapour trail
and the milky way's stigmata.

To Mary over the ferry
a single ticket taken:
to Veronica her sky print veil,
to the water woman a daughter.

The parish church of St Saviour and St Mary Overie (later Southwark Cathedral),
located in an area traditionally best known for its brothels.

Apprentice

Come with me, though the wave is wild
Shelley, 'To William Shelley'

His hair is a flag and openly like fields
    he faces the coming water. His mind fills
with floating pieces of the jigsaw, bridges,
    reaches, signals, wharves, night knowledge.

His father will tell him what to remember:
    not the hard hand of the wind in December
but the days of colliers loaded with labour;
    not the cave or gap at the foot of the ladder

but nights on the jetty watching for ships from Greece.
    The river doesn't scare him with its deep-set looks,
its endlessly provisional position –
    he stands on the steel, a still point round which

things burn or float to sea. Canary Wharf is crowned
    in polar cloud, Limehouse is Table Mountain.
The freemen passing test him on the radio
    to check the things he maybe does not know.

How you can leave one day and not come back again,
    how certain things are taken and certain things remain.

Silvertown

Where the street was a valley
and each ship in its turn
a colossus or cliff at the mouth

out of which you might dream
you could slip like a sea-going question
or Lemuel Gulliver longing for more.

But the sun was our gold, thrown down
for the children to catch as they could
between shadows for hopscotch

and scars cast by derricks and spars,
and at full moon the alleys were paved
with something like silver

then the lines became threads
just powerful enough to tie a man down
and the ship seemed to shrink

become part of the sky
with its far away stars to navigate by
and tell us just where we were now –
the hammer, the pan, the plough.

Last Frost Fair

I should like to know what there is beneath us
Lieut. H.R. Bowers, Antarctica 1912

Lower Hope Point: brought away by the pull
of the moon, glass slides towards the east.
Up at Blackfriars the ice remains solid and silent,
like something completed or maybe about to begin.

In the opium dawn see how the air falls through
to the other side of nothing and survives.
Is it not amazing how the man continues to write?
Remarkably fine here on this limitless snow plain.

He dreams they are roasting a sheep, that someone
has driven a coach and four down from Queenhithe
and right through the tent. We have sandpapered
the runners, this has made a tremendous difference.

At the plying places wherrymen clear the way
for walking on water and the talk is all of the plumber
who ventured to cross with the lead in his hands.
The lord only knows how deep these chasms go.

Clairvoyants gaze at the accidents formed in the frost
while printers' boys carve their names in the monument
of the ice, sell papers to punters to prove they were there
at the last winter fair on the white village green

with its swingboats and puppet-shows, streamers
and flags like an army waved off to a war.
This afternoon 5.2 miles. The writing on the water.
The ash-strewn paths. Your name here.

Cooling

for Keiren

In from the Scandinavias
the vast blank bandages haul
up the deep cut of the tideway

tomorrow's sagas emerging
through numberless mornings
of mist, page after page.

Beneath the city's amber chains
a brotherhood of barges waits
like hot metal cooling, destination

not yet known, swings on the hinge
of slack water, opening, closing,
prepares to face the other way.

Elsewhere a man makes ready
to take his small boat home, out
across the musculature of mud.

Like his father before him
he's watching for the whaleback
of the tide to take him down

toward Shivering Sand, the sea ahead
a pile of stories waiting to be read.

City

for M.H.

The design of lower windows
suggests that their sun shone upwards
towards the surface of the water

their slipways of light emerging
from cellars of half-finished sentences
and dreams of wealthy philanthropists.

Towards the estuary it is possible to make out
the remains of several fishermen's huts
thrown up no doubt in the cataclysm

along with fragments of netting and sky,
and in one place the cast of the unfinished space
between a woman's hands is clearly visible.

Tide

The Earl of Essex's locks of hair are on loan to the Tower of London and will be back on display in April

The National Trust, Ham House

Recalled through the looking-glass plane
to the other side of the water, you wake
on an anti-material pillow of stone

to a polar bear miming in chains,
the unbearable ravens, her majesty's
smack on the face again and again.

No hope that by hanging around
near the countrified jetties and orangeries
you'd escape the black hole of the city

the groans of the moat at the fall of the tide
the unobserved blows to the nape of the neck,
the hour when one becomes minus one.

You've been told you'll be back in the spring.
But try as you might you cannot make out
exactly the spot where the whole thing reverses,

the river, the objects, the life behind glass.

Channel

The water comes and goes over itself – nine miles down then eight and a half back up again

> the water is a puzzle
>> *a reek* <
> which takes a lot
>> *of salt* <
> of thought
>> *and mud* <
> to bring in goods
>> *seaweed* <
> take away goods
>> *and nameless jetsam* <
> and take water for cooling
>> *lovely jubbly* <
> they took turns
>> *it's not so much now* <
> rather like taxi drivers
>> *because they've killed it* <
> put it into boats and took it
>> *in smears of darkness* <
> to a place called the Black Deep
>> *a chaplet of lights* <
> I've seen that boat
>> *growing less* <
> going past
>> *decipherable* <

> a few times
>> *every* <
>> *moment* <

Waterman

It's all finished. There's only one boat out, and that's us

In his eyes it is all winter,
the water stopped like a glacier,
the men's skin grey, hearts frozen
like compass needles at the moment of the crime,
the boat locked in its repeating chapter
from the old boat story, and at the edge
like a series of tasks, the riverbank
struggling to make its way upstream.

It begins as with razors

The lightermen used to buy their pipes pre-packed, then throw them overboard. Not so many of us smoke now

It begins as with razors or lighters,
its sharpness or fire akin to a ship
that is passing, a fragment or sample
of something much bigger and further away
such as fathomless caverns of silver,
whole acres of indigo, saffron or hemp
or hillside on hillside of spices or tea
laid out like a rug to lie down on and sleep.
By capping the bowl like the door
to a furnace some made it last longer,
run cooler for breathing in deeper
its skyfuls of clouds, so that burdens
grown lighter could rise in the water
like palaces turning to smoke,
for a pipe once alight is a dream
which is now or is never and ends
like a pile of disposable bones
washed up on the foreshore
where in the same place the body
of a river ran just hours before.

Here they come

What odd things people throw away from ships
E. Arnot Robinson, *Thames Portrait*

Here they come each leading the other forward
down the green lit corridor to the one-way ward

the battered sun-hat and the half a Pierrot's costume
pale arms flailing for the memory of how to swim

the stricken deckchair and the books, split-hinged
and lost, all bearings that they ever had on anything.

The abandoned lengths of prostrate Baltic timber,
the waving shirt so like a white flag at a window.

Like articles thrown for good to the back of the mind
they circle each other on the bedlam of the ebbing tide

and as they float each views both riverbed and sky.
It is a meditation, like torn sails after a long journey.

River

Call it night, of the sort
with no edges or face
or reflection, a fault-line
of sleeplessness stirring
in tunnels and porches of churches,
a vessel for persons
gone missing or ready to go.

Call it fire, of the kind
which refuses to stop after curfew,
which rips through the heart of the city
from neckline to navel
then spreads through the streets
like the lines of a play
that everyone knows ends in death.

Call it plague, of the type
with no signposts, a secret invasion
down blackened-out streets infected
with fear, a fast-flowing rumour,
a shadow which lives
in the bloodstream, the night-time
which runs through the day.